AF228562

Hawai'i Volcanoes
National Park

by Grace Hansen

abdobooks.com

Published by Abdo Kids, a division of ABDO, P.O. Box 398166, Minneapolis, Minnesota 55439.
Copyright © 2019 by Abdo Consulting Group, Inc. International copyrights reserved in all countries.
No part of this book may be reproduced in any form without written permission from the publisher.
Abdo Kids Jumbo™ is a trademark and logo of Abdo Kids.

Printed in China

102018

012019

Photo Credits: Alamy, iStock, National Park Service, Shutterstock

Production Contributors: Teddy Borth, Jennie Forsberg, Grace Hansen

Design Contributors: Dorothy Toth, Laura Mitchell

Library of Congress Control Number: 2018946218
Publisher's Cataloging-in-Publication Data
Names: Hansen, Grace, author.
Title: Hawai'i Volcanoes National Park / by Grace Hansen.
Description: Minneapolis, Minnesota : Abdo Kids, 2019 | Series: National parks
    Includes glossary, index and online resources (page 24).
Identifiers: ISBN 9781532182082 (lib. bdg.) | ISBN 9781532183065 (ebook) |
    ISBN 9781532183553 (Read-to-me ebook)
Subjects: LCSH: Hawaii Volcanoes National Park (Hawaii)--Juvenile literature. |
    National parks and reserves--Juvenile literature. | Hawaii National Park
    (Hawaii)--Juvenile literature. | Volcanoes--Hawaii--Juvenile literature.
Classification: DDC 996.9--dc23

Table of Contents

Hawai'i Volcanoes National Park

Hawai'i Volcanoes National Park is in Hawaii. It is located in the state's largest island, often called the Big Island.

Conservationists Lorrin
Thurston and Dr. Thomas A.
Jaggar worked to protect
the land. It became the 13th
national park on August 1, 1916.
President Woodrow Wilson
signed it into law.

Nature & Natural Features

Elevations in the park range from sea level to the top of the largest active volcano on Earth. Mauna Loa soars 13,679 feet (4,169 m) high.

9

Along the coast, certain ferns grow from the cracks in hardened lava. Green turtles and the rare hawksbill turtles nest near the sea.

The Hawaiian goose, or the nēnē, is the official state bird. It mainly lives in the park's lowlands.

13

At mid-**elevation** Hawaii's famous 'ohi'a trees grow. The trees bloom beautiful orange-red or yellow flowers. **Native** birds depend on the flowers for **nectar**.

Hawaiian tree ferns grow

in the park's rain forests.

These incredible trees can

only be found in Hawaii.

17

There is only one land mammal native to the park and Hawaii. The Hawaiian hoary bat roosts in large trees. It can be found at almost every elevation.

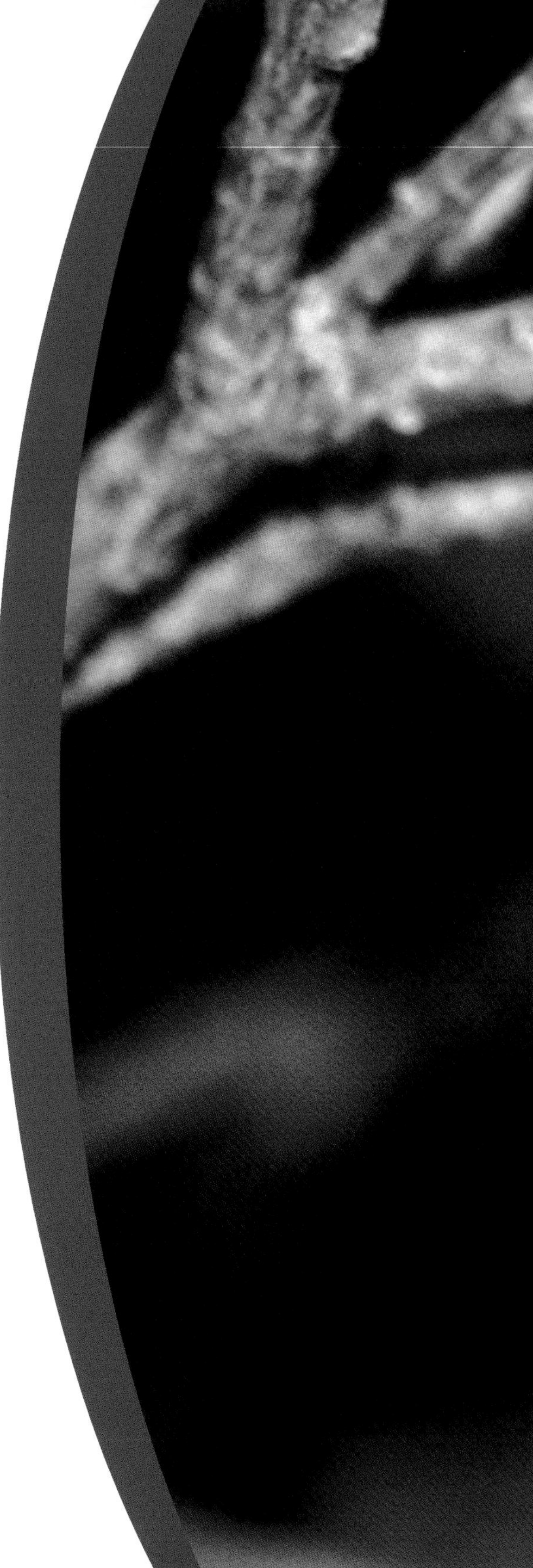

19

Kīlauea is an active shield

volcano in the park. It is

the most active of the five

volcanoes on the island.

20

Fun Activities

Enjoy cultural activities, like learning to make Lei Haku

Explore Nahuku, a 500-year-old lava tube on Kilauea Crater!

Join a guided hike through areas of the park

Take in ocean views and the beloved native Hawaiian monk seals

Glossary

conservationist – a person who acts to protect the environment and wildlife.

elevation – the height above sea level.

mammal – a warm-blooded animal with fur or hair on its skin and a skeleton inside its body.

native – original to.

nectar – the sweet liquid a plant makes.

roost – to rest on a perch.

shield volcano – a volcano that lies low to the ground, resembling a warrior's shield.

23

Index

Visit **abdokids.com** and use this code to access crafts, games, videos, and more!